GW00372039

Yearbook *1994*

L A N D S C A P E S   F R O M

T H E   U L S T E R   M U S E U M

First published by the Appletree Press Ltd.,
19-21 Alfred Street, Belfast BT2 8DL. Text ©
Martyn Anglesea, 1993. Photographs
reproduced with the kind permission of the
Trustees of the Ulster Museum. Printed in
the EC. All rights reserved. No part of this
publication may be reproduced or
transmitted in any form or by any means,
electronic or mechanical, photocopying,
recording or in any information or retrieval
system, without prior permission in writing
from the publishers.

Front cover: The Fox (John Luke)
Back cover: Dunluce Castle (Andrew Nicholl)

ISBN 0-86281-434-0

Foreword

Both in oils and watercolours, the Ulster Museum's collection of paintings is particularly rich in landscapes. It is fitting that Appletree Press has decided this year to vary its well-established yearbook format with a selection from the museum's collection. Because of sustained pressure from the Belfast Art Society and the Ulster Art Club, the first public art gallery in Belfast was set up in 1890 on the top floor of the newly built Central Reference Library in Royal Avenue. Collecting pictures remained piecemeal until the transfer of the entire museum stock to the new building in the Botanic Gardens in 1928. In 1930 Sir John Lavery presented the museum with thirty of his own paintings. Under successive Keepers of Art, the collections of international contemporary art and, in particular, Irish and British art, have been and continue to be steadily built up. With the Museums Act (Northern Ireland) of 1961, the Belfast Museum and Art Gallery was reconstituted as a national museum and became the Ulster Museum. In 1968 a major new extension was begun, which opened to the public in 1972. While it does not limit itself to Ireland, the selection of landscape paintings in this yearbook has, naturally, a bias towards Irish views and Irish artists.

List of Illustrations

List of Illustrations

MONDAY **27**

THURSDAY **30**

TUESDAY **28**

FRIDAY **31**

WEDNESDAY **29**

SATURDAY/SUNDAY **1/2**
New Year's Day

WINTER ABOVE LIGONIEL. *Frederick W. Hull* (born Drogheda 1867; died Belfast 1953). *Oil on board.*

Fred Hull worked as a businessman in Belfast, living at 8 Ireton Street, Botanic Avenue, for more than fifty years. He took up painting as a hobby when about thirty, when he attended evening classes at the Government School of Design under George Trobridge, and took lessons outdoors with David Gould. An early member of the Ulster Arts Club, he exhibited there and at the Royal Hibernian Academy in Dublin. The Lagan Valley was his favourite painting locality. He died in the Royal Victoria Hospital, Belfast. The Ulster Museum has two oil paintings and seven etchings by Hull, and a portrait of him by Paul Nietsche.

MONDAY	3	THURSDAY	6
TUESDAY	4	FRIDAY	7
WEDNESDAY	5	SATURDAY/SUNDAY	8 / 9

SEAGULL ISLE, PORTCOON: 1828. *Andrew Nicholl* (born Belfast 1804; died London 1886). *Watercolour on white paper.*

Even in the early series of watercolour views of the Antrim Coast, the young and inexperienced Nicholl occasionally varied his calm, clear style with an attempt to depict stormy weather. He was later to become much more expert at this, but here we have a good early try. Portcoon is a bay in the basalt cliffs west of the Giant's Causeway. The basalt stack or pillar has been formed by the constant battering and erosion of the cliffs by the sea. Already Nicholl has learnt the trick of scraping out the white shapes of gulls with the point of a sharp knife.

MONDAY	**10**	THURSDAY	**13**
TUESDAY	**11**	FRIDAY	**14**
WEDNESDAY	**12**	SATURDAY/SUNDAY	**15 / 16**

CORSICAN VILLAGE SQUARE, WINTER: 1929.
Herbert H. Newton (born London 1881; died London 1959). *Oil on canvas.*

This artist started life as a businessman in New York, during which time he travelled much in North America, the West Indies and the Far East. After serving in the First World War, he showed some drawings made in Switzerland to the Slade Professor, Henry Tonks, who immediately offered him a place at the Slade School, which he declined. He received some drawing lessons from Leon Underwood, but was self-taught as a painter. Newton visited Corsica in 1929. The view is of the village square of Piana, on the west coast of the island, between Calenzana and Ajaccio.

MONDAY	**17**	THURSDAY	**20**
TUESDAY	**18**	FRIDAY	**21**
WEDNESDAY	**19**	SATURDAY/SUNDAY	**22 / 23**

TOBAR PÁDRAIG, CO. MAYO: 1925. *Eva Henrietta Hamilton* (born Dublin 1876; died Dublin 1960). *Oil on board.*

She was the elder sister of Letitia Hamilton, and was related also to the watercolourist Rose Barton. Both Hamilton sisters studied at the Metropolitan School of Art, Dublin, where they were much influenced by William Orpen. Early in her career Eva was compelled by economic necessity to paint portraits, but later on she turned increasingly to landscape. This broadly painted little seascape study came from the collection of Dr R.I. Best, bequeathed to the museum through the friends of the National Collections of Ireland in 1959.

MONDAY	24	THURSDAY	27
TUESDAY	25	FRIDAY	28
WEDNESDAY	26	SATURDAY/SUNDAY	29 / 30

SUNRISE ON THE ROAD: c 1920. *Sir George Clausen*
(born London 1852; died Newbury, Berkshire, 1944).
Oil on canvas.

Clausen visited Belgium and Holland between 1875 and 1876 and was greatly influenced by Bastien-Lepage and the French plein-air painters, becoming their foremost English disciple. This is a typical example of Clausen's small paintings of the 1920s. It was in the collection of Lord Blanesborough, who admired the artist's misty sunrises and sunsets and became an important patron and friend. Clausen was in the habit of making lightning watercolour sketches of fleeting atmospheric effects, both indoors and outdoors, setting down what he saw and leaving it as soon as he was satisfied that he had all the information that he needed. Having "found" his subject, he then developed the idea in his studio as far as he wished.

MONDAY	**31**	THURSDAY	**3**
TUESDAY	**1**	FRIDAY	**4**
WEDNESDAY	**2**	SATURDAY/SUNDAY	**5/6**

DUNLUCE CASTLE: after 1835. *Andrew Nicholl* (born Belfast 1804; died London 1886). *Watercolour on white paper.*

Andrew Nicholl painted many views of the spectacular old MacDonnell castle on its basalt perch off the north coast of Antrim. Nicholl's mature watercolour style is quite different from his early work. His later watercolours can be very large, and show the influence of the English painters Turner and Copley Fielding. He acquired a repertoire of technical tricks, such as scraping out waves and spray with a knife or the end of a brush. He became more interested in stormy weather, and often exaggerated the height of cliffs for romantic effect.

Clarke

| MONDAY | 7 | THURSDAY | 10 |

| TUESDAY | 8 | FRIDAY | 11 |

| WEDNESDAY | 9 | SATURDAY/SUNDAY | 12 / 13 |

FORESTRY PLANTATION, WINTER: 1965. *Carey Clarke* (born Dublin 1938). *Oil on canvas.*

This painter studied at the National College of Art in Dublin and at the Salzburg Academy in Austria. From the early 1960s he has taught occasionally at the National College of Art. This scene in the Dublin or Wicklow Mountains was exhibited in the Royal Hibernian Academy in 1965 and was presented to the Museum by the Haverty Trust the following year. Though formalised and simplified, the landscape is recognisably that of the Dublin-Wicklow area. Carey Clarke is currently President of the Royal Hibernian Academy.

MONDAY	**14**	THURSDAY	**17**
TUESDAY	**15**	FRIDAY	**18**
WEDNESDAY	**16**	SATURDAY/SUNDAY	**19 / 20**

VIEW OF WARINGSTOWN, CO. DOWN. *Hugh Frazer* (born Dromore, Co. Down, c 1795; died 1861). *Oil on canvas.*

Details about Frazer's life are still somewhat sketchy. In his lifetime he was held in such regard as to be elected in 1836 as president of the short-lived Belfast Association of Artists, and to serve from 1839 to 1853 as Professor of Painting in the Royal Hibernian Academy. This is by far the most attractive of his few identified paintings. The scene is close to Frazer's home town of Dromore, and is dominated by the tower of the seventeenth-century parish church, one of the most interesting examples of "Planters' Gothic" In Ulster. The handling recalls the work of John Constable, whom Frazer evidently admired.

MONDAY	21	THURSDAY	24
TUESDAY	22	FRIDAY	25
WEDNESDAY	23	SATURDAY/SUNDAY	26 / 27

LANDSCAPE NEAR FALCARRAGH, CO. DONEGAL:

c 1900. **William Percy French** (born Cloonyquin, Co. Roscommon, 1854; died Formby, Lancashire, 1920). *Watercolour and bodycolour on white paper.*

With few exceptions, Percy French's watercolours depict bog scenes in the midlands or west of Ireland. Primarily known as an entertainer and writer of comic and sentimental songs, Percy French was also a watercolour painter of somewhat *limited talent. The son of a landowner, he was educated at Windermere College and at Foyle College, then at Trinity College, Dublin, where he qualified as an engineer. He moved to London in 1890, but was soon successful as a performer and toured Canada, the USA and the West Indies. His songs, such as "Phil the Fluter's Ball", "Slattery's Mounted Foot" and "The Mountains of Mourne" are still popular.*

MONDAY	28	THURSDAY	3
TUESDAY	1	FRIDAY	4
WEDNESDAY	2	SATURDAY/SUNDAY	5/6

SUN THROUGH THE WOOD: c 1932. *Ethelbert White* (born Isleworth, Middlesex, 1891; died 1972). *Oil on canvas.*

White studied at the St John's Wood School of Art under Leonard Walker between 1911 and 1912, and exhibited with the London Group from 1916, in which year he was elected a member. From 1916 he also exhibited with the New English Art Club, becoming a member in 1921. White travelled for a number of years around Ireland, the south of France and Spain, but much of his work was done in England, which he explored in nomadic fashion, living in a caravan. Among the books which he illustrated with wood-engravings are Richard Jeffries's The Story of My Heart *(1923) and the Penguin edition of H.D. Thoreau's* Walden. *As an artist he seems to belong among other English ruralists like the Nash brothers, Thomas Hennell and Gilbert Spencer.*

MONDAY	**7**	THURSDAY	**10**
TUESDAY	**8**	FRIDAY	**11**
WEDNESDAY	**9**	SATURDAY/SUNDAY	**12 / 13**

GYPSY ENCAMPMENT ON THE CURRAGH. *Joseph Malachy Kavanagh* (born Dublin 1856; died Dublin 1918). *Oil on canvas.*

Kavanagh received his training in the Royal Hibernian Academy's Schools and in Antwerp under Charles Verlat, along with Walter Osborne and Nathaniel Hill. From 1885 to 1887 he lived in Brittany before returning to Ireland, where he continued a lifelong association with the RHA. He taught in its schools from 1887, and in 1910 was appointed keeper. Probably the foremost exponent of academic Irish landscape painting of his time, Kavanagh was a subtle renderer of transient light and weather effects, as in this spacious view of the Curragh of Co. Kildare. It would have been painted in the studio, not out of doors. The panoramic composition with a big sky is found in seventeenth-century Dutch painters such as Phillips Koninck.

MONDAY	**14**	THURSDAY	**17**
		St Patrick's Day	
TUESDAY	**15**	FRIDAY	**18**
WEDNESDAY	**16**	SATURDAY/SUNDAY	**19 / 20**

McART'S FORT FROM THE MOUNTAIN TO
BETWEEN THE FORT AND THE CANVAS: 1828.

Andrew Nicholl (born Belfast 1804; died London 1886). *Watercolour on white paper.*

This is one of a series of 113 watercolour views of the Antrim Coast, which are Nicholl's earliest datable work, two of them being dated 1828. Nicholl rarely dated his watercolours. At this time he would have been about twenty-four and still *working as a compositor with a Belfast printer. McArt's Fort crowns the summit of Cave Hill, the distinctive basalt cliff which overlooks Belfast from the north. The view looks south across the Lough towards the hills of Co. Down. The fields to the left are now covered by the built-up areas of Fortwilliam and Cliftonville.*

MONDAY	**21**	THURSDAY	**24**
TUESDAY	**22**	FRIDAY	**25**
WEDNESDAY	**23**	SATURDAY/SUNDAY	**26 / 27**

RAILWAY EMBANKMENT. *William John Leech* (born Dublin 1881; died Guildford, Surrey, 1968). *Oil on canvas.*

The son of a professor of law, Leech attended St Columba's College and the Dublin Municipal School of Art, and studied at the Royal Hibernian Academy under Walter Osborne, 1899-1901. He then went to Paris to study at the Académie Julian. He was elected ARHA in 1907 and RHA in 1910. Between 1903 and 1916, Leech lived mainly in Brittany, but exhibited in Dublin from 1907 to 1910 with a group including the Marcievicz couple, George Russell, Percy Gethin and Dermod O'Brien. Leech's painting method was broad, direct and based on the objective rendering of a real place on the spot. It is obvious that this mundane view was painted in the open air.

MONDAY	28	THURSDAY	31

TUESDAY	29	FRIDAY	1
		Good Friday	

WEDNESDAY	30	SATURDAY/SUNDAY	2 / 3
		Easter Sunday	

DAWN, KILLARY HARBOUR: c 1922. *Paul Henry* (born Belfast 1876; died Bray, Co. Wicklow, 1958). *Oil on canvas.*

One of the most successful painters to have come from Belfast, Paul Henry was one of four sons of a Baptist minister. His cousin paid for him to study at the Académie Julian in Paris about 1899-1900. In Paris he met Grace Mitchell, whom he married in 1903. Between 1900 and 1912 he lived mostly in London and was much influenced by Whistler and the post-impressionists. In 1910 he first visited Achill Island, Co. Mayo, which was to become his favourite painting ground. Henry rarely dated his paintings and was vague about chronology, but this was painted about 1922. Probably unknowingly, Henry suffered all his life from red-green colour blindness, which accounts for the restricted palette of this beautiful landscape of western Mayo.

MONDAY 4
Easter Monday

THURSDAY 7

TUESDAY 5

FRIDAY 8

WEDNESDAY 6

SATURDAY/SUNDAY 9 / 10

CASTLE ARCHDALE ON LOUGH ERNE, CO. FERMANAGH: c 1812. *Francis Danby* (born Wexford 1793; died Exmouth, Devon, 1861). *Watercolour on white wove paper.*

Though trained in Dublin, Francis Danby left Ireland in 1813, never to return. He settled in Bristol, where he became the leader of a regional school of painters, and later worked abroad. His early Irish work is very rare. This is the only one of a set of four early Danby watercolours which represents a view in Ulster. The house built by Colonel Mervyn Archdale in 1773 is seen at an angle from near the lake. Since 1959 this house has been derelict. This straightforward, sober watercolour style makes a marked contrast with Danby's later work, which tends to be extravagantly imaginative.

MONDAY	11	THURSDAY	14
TUESDAY	12	FRIDAY	15
WEDNESDAY	13	SATURDAY/SUNDAY	16 / 17

SPRING IN THE TROSSACHS: 1890-91. *David Farquharson* (born Perth 1839; died Birnham 1907)). *Oil on canvas.*

This bright scene of blossoming cherry trees on the banks of a picturesque Perthshire river dates from a time when Farquharson's earlier tight style was loosening and becoming more confident and free. The artist was elected an Associate of the Royal Scottish Academy in 1882 and moved to London four years later. However, he continued to find his subject matter in Scottish landscape. He was working in the neighbourhood of Callender in 1890.

MONDAY	**18**	THURSDAY	**21**
TUESDAY	**19**	FRIDAY	**22**
WEDNESDAY	**20**	SATURDAY/SUNDAY	**23 / 24**

THE FOX: 1937. *John Luke* (born Belfast 1906; died Belfast 1975). *Oil and tempera on panel.*

After leaving the Slade School of Art in 1931, John Luke developed the careful drawing style he had learnt there under Henry Tonks into his own distinctive tempera technique. In provincial Belfast, this was considered startlingly modern. It was, however, admired by the young poet John Hewitt, who was in charge of art at the Belfast Museum, and became a friend and patron of Luke. This is a landscape of the imagination, the colours of which are not based on nature. Like most of Luke's mature paintings, the composition was closely worked out through pencil outlines, and the picture painstakingly built up in layers of thin water-based tempera paint. For many years Luke taught the life classes at Belfast College of Art, and was revered by generations of students for his obsessional exactitude and concentration.

MONDAY	25	THURSDAY	28
TUESDAY	26	FRIDAY	29
WEDNESDAY	27	SATURDAY/SUNDAY	30 / 1

A BANK OF FLOWERS, WITH A VIEW OF BRAY, CO. WICKLOW: after 1835. *Andrew Nicholl* (born Belfast 1804; died London 1886). *Watercolour on white paper.*

During the second half of the 1830s Andrew Nicholl lived for some time in Dublin, where he appears to have conceived his most attractive compositions, these distant views seen through a bank of wild flowers. This one is actually inscribed on the back: "Summer wild flowers: Bray and the Valley of the Dargle from Killiney Hill, Co. Dublin". The delicate white sprays of cow-parsley are drawn with the tip of a sharp knife, scraping away the darker paint and exposing the white paper beneath. Other similar Irish views are known, including Derry, Carrickfergus and the White Rocks at Portrush.

MONDAY	2	THURSDAY	5
TUESDAY	3	FRIDAY	6
WEDNESDAY	4	SATURDAY/SUNDAY	7/8

DAN NANCY'S, CUSHENDUN: 1933. *Romeo Charles Toogood* (born Belfast 1902; died Belfast 1966). *Oil on canvas.*

Having worked as a painter and decorator, Romeo Toogood studied at the Belfast School of Art and the Royal College of Art, and after serving as art master in several Ulster schools was appointed painting and drawing master at the Belfast College of Art. Here his many pupils included T.P. Flanagan, Basil Blackshaw and Cherith Boyd. This is an early painting of a scene in the Glens of Antrim above Cushendun, where the steep road was called "Dan Nancy's Brae" after the owner of the upper farm, Dan (Nancy) McKay. It was made from watercolours painted on the spot while on holiday in the summer of 1933. Toogood's style at this time was quite broad. Later, possibly under the influence of his colleague John Luke, his paintings became harder and flatter in their outlines.

MONDAY	**9**	THURSDAY	**12**
TUESDAY	**10**	FRIDAY	**13**
WEDNESDAY	**11**	SATURDAY/SUNDAY	**14 / 15**

THE CHERRY ORCHARD. *John Clayton Adams* (born Ewhurst Hill, Guildford, Surrey, 1840; died Guildford 1906). *Oil on canvas.*

This landscape painter of southern England sent work to the Royal Academy between 1863 and 1904 and also exhibited with the New Water-Colour Society. Much of his work celebrates the pastoral landscape of his native Surrey, which, though close to London, remained wild and undeveloped until the encroachment of suburbia early this century. This was because the land was comparatively poor for farming. The Victorians found in Surrey an untamed, Scottish-looking terrain in easy reach of the metropolis.

MONDAY	**16**	THURSDAY	**19**
TUESDAY	**17**	FRIDAY	**20**
WEDNESDAY	**18**	SATURDAY/SUNDAY	**21 / 22**

THE RED CART: c 1946. *Maurice MacGonigal* (born Dublin 1900; died Dublin 1979). *Oil on plywood panel.*

This was painted between 1945 and 1947 when MacGonigal stayed with his family at Carraroe, a Gaeltacht area of Co. Galway. The place depicted was called Bothar Buidhe, or the yellow road. When painting landscapes, MacGonigal usually worked directly from the scene in front of him, but also made drawings and watercolour notes to remind himself of features to integrate in the picture later on, in his studio. MacGonigal taught for many years at the National College of Art in Dublin, and served as President of the Royal Hibernian Academy from 1962 to 1977.

MONDAY	**23**	THURSDAY	**26**
TUESDAY	**24**	FRIDAY	**27**
WEDNESDAY	**25**	SATURDAY/SUNDAY	**28 / 29**

TURF BOG, CONNEMARA. *James Humbert Craig*

(born Belfast 1878; died Cushendun, Co. Antrim, 1944).

Oil on canvas.

This painting was acquired by exchange from the artist's widow in 1945. While Paul Henry was the first Irish painter to discover the potential of Connemara as a painting locality, Humbert Craig quickly followed him there. This kind of bog landscape with turf stacks was frequently treated by Henry.

Though he painted a great deal in Connemara and Donegal, Craig's favourite area was the Glens of Antrim which continually prompted his return.

MONDAY	**30**	THURSDAY	**2**
TUESDAY	**31**	FRIDAY	**3**
WEDNESDAY	**1**	SATURDAY/SUNDAY	**4 / 5**

A SUMMER DAY ON THE THAMES: c 1930. *James Humbert Craig* (born Belfast 1878; died Cushendun, Co. Antrim, 1944). *Oil on canvas.*

As this undated small painting was bought by the Museum in 1931, it is reasonable to assume that it had been painted recently. With Paul Henry and others, Craig participated in a group exhibition of Irish artists at the Fine Art Society, London, in 1928. He also exhibited at the Royal Academy. He travelled and painted in Switzerland, France and Spain. English scenes by Humbert Craig are rare. This was evidently painted on the spot at a boating resort somewhere along the Thames.

June   *1994*

MONDAY	**6**	THURSDAY	**9**
TUESDAY	**7**	FRIDAY	**10**
WEDNESDAY	**8**	SATURDAY/SUNDAY	**11 / 12**

RIVER IN THE SAND: 1924. *George William Russell ("AE")* (born Lurgan, Co. Armagh, 1867; died Bournemouth 1935). *Oil on canvas.*

One of the leading literary figures in the Irish Cultural Renaissance, George Russell was a "myriad-minded man", working by turns as poet, painter, writer, agriculturalist, visionary and mystic. This was painted in Donegal in the summer of 1924 and presented by the artist to the Belfast Museum in November that year "as an Ulsterman in token of friendship to Ulster". He also gave instructions that it should be framed in a simple "Whistler frame". While many of AE's paintings have an elemental or fairy content, this is an objective piece of broadly painted landscape, peopled by two small boys, not fairies.

MONDAY	**13**	THURSDAY	**16**
TUESDAY	**14**	FRIDAY	**17**
WEDNESDAY	**15**	SATURDAY/SUNDAY	**18 / 19**

VILLAGE BY THE SEA: 1953. *Norah Allison McGuinness* (born Londonderry 1903; died Dublin 1980). *Oil on canvas.*

Daughter of a Derry coal merchant and shipowner, Norah McGuinness entered the Metropolitan School of Art, Dublin, in 1921. Here she studied under Patrick Tuohy, Oswald Reeves and Harry Clarke. On the advice of Mainie Jellett, she went to Paris and studied under André Lhote, 1929-31, but his frigid academic cubism failed to influence her. After a short period in America, she returned to Ireland permanently in 1939. Her work at this time, mainly landscape and townscape, was inspired by the work of the French Fauves of thirty years before. In 1944 she succeeded Mainie Jellett as President of the Irish Exhibition of Living Art. This was painted in 1953 in the harbour village of Dunmore East, Co. Waterford, and was lent by the artist to the Irish Exhibition of Living Art that year.

| MONDAY | 4 | THURSDAY | 7 |

| TUESDAY | 5 | FRIDAY | 8 |

| WEDNESDAY | 6 | SATURDAY/SUNDAY | 9 / 10 |

THE SIERRA NEVADA, GRANADA, SPAIN: 1921.
Jane de Glehn (born Jane Erin Emmett, Pelham, New York, 1873; died Stratford Tony, Wiltshire, 1957). *Oil on canvas.*

This Irish-American painter studied in New York under William Merrit Chase and Frederick MacMonnies. In 1903 she met the English painter Wilfred de Glehn, who was visiting New York with his friend John Singer Sargent. She married de Glehn the following year. Settling in Chelsea, London, they travelled widely and exhibited on both sides of the Atlantic. This Spanish view, exhibited at the Royal Academy in 1921, shows the simplified, boldly brushed style associated with Sargent and his circle, the English and American Impressionists.

MONDAY	**11**	THURSDAY	**14**
TUESDAY	**12**	FRIDAY	**15**
WEDNESDAY	**13**	SATURDAY/SUNDAY	**16 / 17**

THE BRIDGE AT GREZ: 1901. *Sir John Lavery* (born Belfast 1856; died Rossenarra, Co. Kilkenny, 1941). *Oil on canvas.*

Lavery migrated from Belfast to Glasgow at an early age, and is usually classified among the group of young Francophile painters known as "the Glasgow Boys". As an art student in Paris he came under the influence of Jean Bastien-Lepage, who believed in painting out of doors on grey days and expressing solidity by painting with a square brush across rather than along the form. The village of Grez-sur-Loing, near Fontainebleau, was then a picturesque and cheap resort for painters, writers and musicians. Its medieval bridge made a splendid subject, and Lavery admitted that he painted it at least ten times. It appears in the background of his large early painting The Cherry Tree *of 1884.*

MONDAY	18	THURSDAY	21
TUESDAY	19	FRIDAY	22
WEDNESDAY	20	SATURDAY/SUNDAY	23 / 24

FIELD OF CORN, PONT AVEN: 1892. *Roderic O'Conor* (born Milton, Co. Roscommon, 1860; died Neuil-sur-Layon 1940). *Oil on canvas.*

Coming from a comfortable Irish landowning background and educated at Amplèforth, Roderic O'Conor enjoyed financial independence which enabled him to settle in France as a young man and to concentrate on painting without economic pressures. He was a member of the circle of post-impressionist painters who congregated around Paul Gauguin in the Breton village of Pont-Aven, where this remarkable little picture was painted. The juxtapositioning of complementary colours reminds us of the work of Van Gogh, who was dead by the time this was painted. As O'Conor deliberately avoided art dealers, his work remained obscure during his lifetime and has been rediscovered only during the last thirty years.

MONDAY	**25**	THURSDAY	**28**
TUESDAY	**26**	FRIDAY	**29**
WEDNESDAY	**27**	SATURDAY/SUNDAY	**30 / 31**

EVENING, BALLYCASTLE: c 1924. *Frank McKelvey* (born Belfast 1895; died Belfast 1974). *Oil on canvas.*

Frank McKelvey was Ulster's primary anti-modernist painter. The son of a painter and decorator, McKelvey designed posters before entering the Belfast School of Art, where he won prizes for figure drawing in 1911 and 1913. Possessed of considerable handskills and sensitive observation, particularly in landscape and seascape in Antrim and Donegal, he worked also as a portrait painter, but accepted rather too many potboiler commissions. He first exhibited at the Royal Hibernian Academy in 1918, and every subsequent year of his life. He was elected ARHA in 1923 and RHA in 1930. In 1931 he was one of the first twelve elected academicians of the Ulster Academy of Arts. In this relatively early painting, the influence of the landscapes of William Russell Flint is apparent.

MONDAY	**1**	THURSDAY	**4**
TUESDAY	**2**	FRIDAY	**5**
WEDNESDAY	**3**	SATURDAY/SUNDAY	**6/7**

OLIVES AT COLLIOURE: 1911. *James Dickson Innes* (born Llanelly, South Wales, 1887; died Swanley, Kent, 1914). *Oil on canvas.*

This Welsh painter attended the Slade School where he adopted the impressionist style of the teacher there, Philip Wilson Steer. Later, under the influence of the French Fauves, he developed a rapid painting method using intoxicating colour. He was a member of the New English Art Club and the Camden Town Group, and travelled widely, sometimes accompanied by his compatriot, Augustus John. This was painted in the south of France, near the Spanish border, in the summer of 1911. Innes visited Collioure and the surrounding area on painting expeditions several times between 1908 and 1912. Never physically robust, Innes died of consumption at the age of twenty-seven.

MONDAY	8	THURSDAY	11
TUESDAY	9	FRIDAY	12
WEDNESDAY	10	SATURDAY/SUNDAY	13 / 14

NEAR ALICANTE, ANDALUSIA, SPAIN: c 1952.
George Campbell (born Arklow, Co. Wicklow, 1917; died Dublin 1979). *Bodycolour on laminated board.*

George Campbell, son of the primitive painter Gretta Bowen, and younger brother of the photographer Arthur Campbell, attended Richview School, Dublin, before the family moved to Belfast. He left commercial work to become a full-time painter, a craft at which he was practically self-taught. George Campbell's first one-man-show was at Victor Waddington's Gallery, Dublin, in 1946. He worked with Gerard Dillon in Connemara, and they lived together and exhibited in London. From about 1950 Campbell spent half of each year in Malaga in southern Spain, where he was recognised as a flamenco guitarist. A brightly coloured scene of peasants working in fields, this must date from the time when Campbell had just begun spending part of the year in Spain.

MONDAY	**15**	THURSDAY	**18**
TUESDAY	**16**	FRIDAY	**19**
WEDNESDAY	**17**	SATURDAY/SUNDAY	**20 / 21**

THE OLD CALLAN BRIDGE, ARMAGH: 1945. *John Luke* (born Belfast 1906; died Belfast 1975). *Oil and tempera on board. Armagh County Museum.*

Because of the air-raids on Belfast in 1941, John Luke and his mother left to live on a farm at Knappagh, Killylea, Co. Armagh. This is a view close to Armagh City, with the tower and pinnacles of the Church of Ireland cathedral showing above the trees. The landscape is painted using Luke's exact tempera style, which he developed himself. It was a slow process, beginning with a careful pencil outline. The modelling would then be built up in monochrome shades of grey. Only after this had been finished and allowed to dry would the final colour be added, built up in layers. As Luke was such a slow, careful worker, the number of finished paintings he produced was not large.

MONDAY	**22**	THURSDAY	**25**
TUESDAY	**23**	FRIDAY	**26**
WEDNESDAY	**24**	SATURDAY/SUNDAY	**27 / 28**

THE WALLS OF MARRAKESH: 1920. *Sir John Lavery* (born Belfast 1856; died Rossenarra, Co. Kilkenny, 1941). *Oil on canvas.*

By the time this was painted, Lavery was well established as a high-society portrait painter, moving easily among his rich and glamorous clients, aided by his beautiful American wife. He had received a knighthood in the New Years Honours list of 1918. He had also acquired a prestigious London studio at 5 Cromwell Place, and a house and studio at Tangier on the Mediterranean coast of Morocco, where he usually spent the winters. The medieval Moorish city of Marrakesh is on the Atlantic coast, south of Casablanca. An inscription on the back of this vibrantly bright painting seems to indicate that it was finished in his London studio.

MONDAY	**29**	THURSDAY	**1**
TUESDAY	**30**	FRIDAY	**2**
WEDNESDAY	**31**	SATURDAY/SUNDAY	**3/4**

HAY HARVEST: 1918. *Alfred Rawlings Baker* (born Southampton 1865; died London 1939). *Oil on canvas.*

Baker studied at the Hartley School of Art, Southampton, and the Académie Julian, Paris, and came to Belfast about 1891 to teach painting at the School of Art. He was vice-president of the Belfast Art Society in 1892–93 and president on two occasions, 1899-1900 and 1915-17. In 1931 he was elected honorary academician of the Ulster Academy of Arts. The Royal Ulster Academy has a self-portrait by Baker. He retired from the Art School in 1934 and may then have returned to England. Baker designed a poster showing "Corfe Castle, Dorset" for Southern Railways. This harvest scene could have been painted in Ireland or England. It was exhibited at the Belfast Art Society in 1918.

MONDAY	**5**	THURSDAY	**8**
TUESDAY	**6**	FRIDAY	**9**
WEDNESDAY	**7**	SATURDAY / SUNDAY	**10 / 11**

SAN VITO ROMANO: 1923. *E.M. O'R. Dickey* (born Belfast 1894; died Colchester, Essex, 1977). *Oil on canvas.*

The son of a Belfast solicitor, Dickey was educated at Wellington and Trinity College, Cambridge. He then studied under Harold Gilman at the Westminster School of Art, and exhibited with the Royal Academy, the New English Art Club and the London Group. Dickey was art master at Oundle School, Northamptonshire, 1924-26, where one of his pupils was Tom Carr. This cleanly handled painting reminds us that in 1920 Dickey was one of the founders of the Society of Wood-Engravers and was an able practitioner of that exacting craft. San Vito is one of the precariously sited little towns on the volcanic hills around Rome.

MONDAY	**12**	THURSDAY	**15**
TUESDAY	**13**	FRIDAY	**16**
WEDNESDAY	**14**	SATURDAY/SUNDAY	**17 / 18**

CARRICK-A-REDE, CO. ANTRIM: 1828. *Andrew Nicholl* (born Belfast 1804; died London 1886). *Watercolour on white paper.*

This is one of the long series of views of the Antrim Coast, which Nicholl painted at the age of about twenty-four. His early, self-taught style employs pencil outlining, clear crisp washes and a certain naivety which he was soon to lose after his first visit to London in 1830. Carrick-a-Rede is a basalt stack near Ballintoy on the north Antrim Coast, where in the summer months the local fishermen erect a precarious rope-bridge for access. In Nicholl's picture the bridge appears to be secured with stay-ropes, which are no longer used.

MONDAY	**19**	THURSDAY	**22**
TUESDAY	**20**	FRIDAY	**23**
WEDNESDAY	**21**	SATURDAY/SUNDAY	**24 / 25**

THE ESTUARY OF THE SHANNON: 1939. *Dermod O'Brien* (born Mount Trenchard, Foynes, Co. Limerick, 1865; died Dublin 1945). *Oil on canvas.*

This was exhibited at the Royal Hibernian Academy in 1939, entitled The Estuary of the Shannon at Foynes. *The village of Foynes, O'Brien's birthplace, was formerly a seaplane base. O'Brien was the longest-serving President of the Royal Hibernian Society, holding that office from 1910 until his death in 1945.*

He was a grandson of William Smith O'Brien, the Young Irelander, and a cousin of Lord Inchiquin. Educated at Harrow and Cambridge, he studied art in Rome, Antwerp and Paris and became a successful portrait painter as well as a generous patron of younger artists.

MONDAY	26	THURSDAY	29
TUESDAY	27	FRIDAY	30
WEDNESDAY	28	SATURDAY/SUNDAY	1/2

MOUNTAIN LANDSCAPE IN WALES: c 1925-30.
Christopher Richard Wynne Nevinson (born Hampstead, London, 1889; died London 1946). *Oil on canvas.*

This painting was bought, at Nevinson's instigation, from John Magee's Belfast Gallery in 1930. By then Nevinson was highly thought of in modern British art circles and was represented in practically every major public collection. At first associated with the Vorticist movement, his traumatic experiences in the trenches in 1915-17 left him disillusioned with avant-garde art and led to his return to naturalistic painting. Though this is basically a naturalistic landscape, it contains traces of Cubist/ Vorticist angularity, particularly in the treatment of the road. The triple peaks in the distance could be the Snowdon massif.

DAVID FULTON R.S.W.

MONDAY	3	THURSDAY	6
TUESDAY	4	FRIDAY	7
WEDNESDAY	5	SATURDAY/SUNDAY	8 / 9

AN AUTUMN MORNING. *David Fulton* (born Glasgow 1848; died Glasgow 1930). *Oil on canvas.*

Fulton was a minor member of the group of artists known as "the Glasgow Boys", who emerged from the Glasgow School of Art in the 1870s and 1880s. The group included Joseph Crawhall, George Henry, D.Y. Cameron, John Lavery and Edward Atkinson Hornel (1864-1933). Though Fulton was a lot older than Hornel, this painting, presumably located on the shores of the Firth of Clyde, shows much similarity in handling to Hornel's work. Occasionally, as here, we find an older artist influenced by a younger one.

MONDAY	**10**	THURSDAY	**13**
TUESDAY	**11**	FRIDAY	**14**
WEDNESDAY	**12**	SATURDAY/SUNDAY	**15 / 16**

THE OLD MILL, HOLYWOOD, CO. DOWN: 1834.

Andrew Nicholl (born Belfast 1804; died London 1886).

Watercolour on white paper.

This is inscribed "sketched August 1834". It is rare for Nicholl to date his watercolours, so his chronology is difficult to establish. This relatively early example postdates his first visit to London in 1830, when he would have seen the work of Copley Fielding and Turner. This transformed his pictorial style. His drawing of cattle had improved, and he had learnt the scraping or sgraffito technique, which he has used to indicate the weeds in the foreground. The old mill stood between Holywood and Bangor. In Nicholl's watercolour it is already derelict. When James Moore sketched it nine years later, in 1843, it was reduced to a pole supporting the mechanism.

Antrim augt 20th 1867

MONDAY	**17**	THURSDAY	**20**
TUESDAY	**18**	FRIDAY	**21**
WEDNESDAY	**19**	SATURDAY/SUNDAY	**22 / 23**

ANTRIM: 20 August 1867. **Dr James Moore** (born Belfast 1819; died Belfast 1883). *Watercolour on white paper.*

Once he had evolved his quick watercolour sketching style, which he did early on while a medical student in Edinburgh, James Moore did not change it. He travelled widely, generally on business connected with his profession as a consultant surgeon, in Ireland, Britain and on the Continent, always taking his watercolour box with him. The Ulster Museum has *over 400 of his sketches, which are now of topographical value as well as artistic quality. This is a rather late example showing the old bridge over the Six Mile Water in Antrim town.*

MONDAY	**24**	THURSDAY	**27**
TUESDAY	**25**	FRIDAY	**28**
WEDNESDAY	**26**	SATURDAY/SUNDAY	**29 / 30**

ON ACHILL ISLAND: 1938. *Charles Lamb* (born Portadown 1893; died Carraroe, Connemara, 1964). *Oil on canvas.*

Originally trained as a house-painter, Charles Lamb attended evening classes at the Belfast School of Art, and in 1917 won a scholarship to the Metropolitan School of Art, Dublin. After four years there, he went to live in a cottage at Carraroe, in a remote part of Connemara. He travelled all over Ireland and exhibited regularly in the Royal Hibernian Academy as well as in London and America. In 1935 Lamb built a house at Carraroe, and founded an annual summer school there. The artist had a horse-drawn caravan, in which he travelled from Carraroe to Achill and back.

Over-flow of the Lagan above the second lock - Nov. 4. 1845.

| MONDAY | **31** | THURSDAY | **3** |

| TUESDAY | **1** | FRIDAY | **4** |

| WEDNESDAY | **2** | SATURDAY/SUNDAY | **5 / 6** |

OVERFLOW ON THE LAGAN ABOVE THE SECOND LOCK: 4 November 1845. **Dr James Moore** (born Belfast 1819; died Belfast 1883). *Watercolour on white wove paper.*

James Moore painted many watercolours along the towpath of what was then the Lagan Canal, which linked Stranmillis in Belfast with Lough Neagh. It was used for transporting bricks and tiles from Coalisland to the port at Belfast. This is the weir above the second lock at Belvoir, known as "Mickey Taylor's", the remains of which can still be seen today. Only the foundations survive of the lock-keeper's cottage, shown by Moore as inhabited. The foliage effect is obtained by dragging an almost-dry brush over the rough texture of the paper.

MONDAY	**7**	THURSDAY	**10**
TUESDAY	**8**	FRIDAY	**11**
WEDNESDAY	**9**	SATURDAY/SUNDAY	**12 / 13**

THE GIANT'S CAUSEWAY FROM THE WEST: after 1835. *Andrew Nicholl* (born Belfast 1804; died London 1886). *Watercolour on white paper.*

This mature watercolour by Andrew Nicholl shows his mastery of the atmospheric tricks of rubbing and scraping, used by painters such as Copley Fielding, to whose work Nicholl's was compared in his lifetime. He was referred to as "the Irish Copley Fielding". The spray of the waves is produced by scraping away the paint with a knife, exposing the white paper beneath. The height of the cliffs and of the Grand Causeway has been exaggerated for romantic effect. The old woman in the red shawl was a local character who sold whiskey to tourists, who were invited to water it at the "Giant's Well" beside which she sits.

November *1994*

MONDAY	**14**	THURSDAY	**17**
TUESDAY	**15**	FRIDAY	**18**
WEDNESDAY	**16**	SATURDAY/SUNDAY	**19 / 20**

LANDSCAPE WITH BANDITTI: c 1755-57. *Richard Wilson* (born Penygoes, Montgomeryshire, Wales, 1713; died Colomendy, Mold, 1782). *Oil on canvas.*

The son of a Welsh clergyman, Wilson had aristocratic connections and established himself as the ideal literary landscape painter of the British ruling class. He was also an able classical scholar and could recite Virgil by heart. He was in Rome for a long period from 1750, where he studied the works of Claude Lorrain and Gaspar Poussin, but this early scene of robbers in a wild Italian landscape recalls rather the work of Salvator Rosa. In 1768, having returned to London, Wilson was one of the founder members of the Royal Academy. Unfortunately, the collapse of his ideals led to drunken decline and he spent his last years with relatives in North Wales.

November

MONDAY **21**

THURSDAY

TUESDAY **22**

FRIDAY **25**

WEDNESDAY **23**

SATURDAY/SUNDAY **26 / 27**

THE FIELD: 1953. *Basil Blackshaw* (born Glengormley, Co. Antrim, 1932; lives in Antrim). *Oil on canvas.*

This is an early expressionistic painting in typically subdued colour by an artist who is now one of Northern Ireland's foremost. Blackshaw was brought up at Boardmills, Co. Down. He attended the Methodist College, Belfast, and Belfast College of Art 1948-51. An early admirer and patron was the poet John Hewitt, who was then Keeper of Art in what is now the Ulster Museum. His work contains many landscape elements, such as Colin Mountain and the Slieve Croob Hills. Horses, dogs and the world of fanciers and breeders form another important part of his subject-matter. He has also painted formal portraits.

MONDAY	28	THURSDAY	1
TUESDAY	29	FRIDAY	2
WEDNESDAY	30	SATURDAY/SUNDAY	3 / 4

A GOOD CATCH, DONEGAL: 1943-44. *James Humbert Craig* (born Belfast 1878; died Cushendun, Co. Antrim, 1944). *Oil on canvas.*

This is the last picture painted by Humbert Craig. It is unfinished and unsigned, as he was still working on it in his studio at Cushendun at the time of his death. It was presented to the Belfast Museum by Craig's widow the following year. Donegal was a favourite painting locality for Craig, who appreciated the constantly changing cloud patterns and the clarity of the light. It could be claimed that three Ulster painters, Craig, Paul Henry and Frank McKelvey, created between them a distinctive school of Irish landscape painting in their annual contributions to the Royal Hibernian Academy exhibitions in Dublin.

MONDAY	5	THURSDAY	8
TUESDAY	6	FRIDAY	9
WEDNESDAY	7	SATURDAY/SUNDAY	10 / 11

WEST VIEW OF PLEASKIN FROM ABOVE: 1828.
Andrew Nicholl (born Belfast 1804; died London 1886).
Watercolour on white paper.

This is a view from the cliff path above Pleaskin Head to the east of the Giant's Causeway, now maintained by the National Trust. Naive though they are, these early watercolours of the north Antrim Coast convey a striking sense of linear design. His drawing of cattle was later to improve. But the successive flows of basalt lava seen in the cliffs are well observed, suggesting that Nicholl possessed an innate sense of geology. Walking along the tops of the cliffs of the Causeway Coast can be in some respects a more spectacular experience than walking on the Causeway itself.

MONDAY	**12**	THURSDAY	**15**
TUESDAY	**13**	FRIDAY	**16**
WEDNESDAY	**14**	SATURDAY/SUNDAY	**17 / 18**

NEWCASTLE PIER: 3 May 1862. **Dr James Moore** (born Belfast 1819; died Belfast 1883). *Watercolour on white paper.*

This is a stormy scene, with boats sheltering behind the breakwater at Newcastle, Co. Down. The trick of scraping out the highlights on the breakers with a knife, revealing the white paper, was presumably learnt by Moore from Andrew Nicholl. Moore's sense of atmospheric colour and aerial perspective rarely fails him. He sketched in watercolour out of doors in all weathers and became a much more proficient spontaneous sketcher from nature than his master Nicholl ever was.

MONDAY 19

THURSDAY 22

TUESDAY 20

FRIDAY 23

WEDNESDAY 21

SATURDAY/SUNDAY 24 / 25
Christmas Eve / Christmas Day

WINTER, CUSHENDUN. *Maurice Canning Wilks*
(born Belfast 1910; died Belfast 1984). *Armagh County
Museum.*

*The son of a linen designer, Maurice Wilks attended Malone
Public Elementary School and went to evening classes at the
Belfast School of Art, where he excelled in life-drawing. A
Dunville Scholarship enabled him to study full-time. He exhibited
first at the Royal Hibernian Academy at the age of nineteen.*

*He exhibited frequently in Dublin, as well as in Canada and the
United States. In landscape painting, Wilks followed in the
footsteps of Humbert Craig, working for a time in the same
village, Cushendun. The landscape of the middle of the Glens
of Antrim, especially Glendun, proved a lasting and saleable
inspiration for both artists.*

December – January

MONDAY **26**

THURSDAY **29**

TUESDAY **27**

FRIDAY **30**

WEDNESDAY **28**

SATURDAY/SUNDAY **31 / 1**

New Year's Day

KNOCKALLA HILLS, CO. DONEGAL: 1951. *Dan O'Neill* (born Belfast 1920; died Belfast 1974). *Oil on masonite panel.*

The Knockalla Mountains are on the Fanad Peninsula in North Donegal, between Carrowkeel and Saldanha Head. In 1945 Dan O'Neill had given up working night-shifts as an electrician and painting at home during the day. With the help of the Dublin dealer Victor Waddington, he was able to exhibit his paintings regularly in Dublin and London, and to paint full-time. Throughout his career O'Neill was associated with two other Belfast painters, George Campbell and Gerard Dillon, both of whom took their main inspiration, as did O'Neill, from Irish landscape and folk-life.

Acknowledgements

The publisher wishes to thank the following for permission to reproduce work in copyright:

Basil Blackshaw (The Field); M. Broughton-Mills and Norah Nicholson (A Good Catch, Turf Bog, Connemara and A Summer Day on the Thames by James Humbert Craig); Carey Clarke (Forestry Plantation, Winter); C.H.B. Cox (Railway Embankment by William John Leech); Mary Dickey (San Vito Romano by E.M. O'R. Dickey); Ciaran MacGonigal (The Red Cart by Maurice MacGonigal); R. McGuinness (Village by the Sea by Norah McGuinness); Sadie McKee (The Old Callan Bridge, The Road to the West and The Fox by John Luke); Robert McKelvey (Evening, Ballycastle by Frank McKelvey); Anthony O'Brien (The Estuary of the Shannon by Dermod O'Brien); Bridget Stalley (Knockalla Hills, Co. Donegal by Dan O'Neill); Anne Toogood (Dan Nancy's, Cushendun by Romeo Toogood); Berry Wilks (Winter, Cushendun by Maurice Wilks).

While every effort has been made to contact copyright holders, the publisher would welcome information on any oversight which may have occurred.